Heal

GW00792794

Flows

Jonathan & Anna

Edwards

We want to thank Alyson Tandy and Astrid Tate for taking the time to proof read this book for us, without their help there would be many spelling mistakes.

The names within this book have been changed to protect individual's personal privacy.

Jonathan & Anna Edwards have asserted their rights under the Copyright, Designs and Patents Act 1988, to be identified as Author of this work

All correspondence to:
J Edwards findyourinsight@gmail.com
www.findyourinsight.com

First published in 2016 ISBN: 978-1-326-73962-1

Contents

Introduction

God heals today, this truth is a reality that many people have experienced, through the power of the Holy Spirit. When you read this book, you will discover that God does not put sickness on humanity, neither does He take delight in suffering or tragedy. He is the God who heals and desires that we live in health.

Through the last two decades, medicine and science has advanced at a tremendous rate. This has resulted in medical science having outstanding results in everything from controlling heart disease, to targeted therapy in cancer treatment, to advancement in HIV research.

We praise God for every doctor, nurse, and medical institution around the world who is engaged in the fight against sickness and disease. This book has not been written to criticise the medical profession, for we see this as one method that God uses to bring health to millions of people around the globe today.

Yet for every new advancement in medicine, there are new diseases emerging all the time, many of them incurable. This is because our world is fallen, increasing in darkness, *(Isaiah 60:2)*, and lost without the gospel of Jesus Christ, *(Ephesians 2:1-5)*.

God is the great physician; His desire is to heal people of all sickness and disease, curable and incurable. In a world where multitudes of humanity have no hope and are without God, *(Ephesians 2:12)* we as believers can turn to the God of all hope, *(Romans 15:13)* and embrace a loving God who is more than willing and able to heal all sickness and disease.

We believe that as you read this book, the Holy Spirit will give you revelation and insight into His plan for health and wholeness. We are praying and believing that this book will be more than information, but transformation and prove to be a great testimony of Gods healing power in your life. As you read this book, your life will never be the same again.

Therefore, please now throw off all preconceived ideas of divine healing; forget what you have been told, allow God to speak to you from his word afresh. For He was and He will forever be the God who heals, *(Exodus 15:26)*.

Chapter One

Is it God's Will to Heal?

There are many questions that people have regarding divine healing.

As my wife and I travel, we have found that many are looking for valid answers to the pain and suffering that they face, these range from:

Does God heal today?

Does He heal some and not others?

Why are some people prayed for and still remain sick?

Why does healing not always happen immediately?

These are very valid questions, and ones that need to be answered firstly from scripture and secondly from personal experience.

We all long and yearn for the day when society experiences healing power as much and as frequent as when Christ walked the earth, for next to scripture, the most convincing argument is always experience.

Jesus answered and said to them, "Go and tell John the things you have seen and heard: that the blind see, the lame walk, the lepers are cleansed, the deaf hear, the dead are raised, the poor have the gospel preached to them.
(Luke 7:22).

When the sun was setting, all those who had any that were sick with various diseases brought them to Him; and He laid His hands on every one of them and healed them.
(Luke 4:40).

I personally believe that what Jesus preached and demonstrated, concerning the will and the nature of God, hasn't changed in two thousand years. Just like He healed all illness and disease then, He is willing to heal all types of sickness and disease now.

Nowhere in the gospels do you find Christ encouraging the sick to live with their illness. On the contrary, He treats sickness as a manifestation of the kingdom of darkness, disease as an enemy, which He was sent to destroy.

How God anointed Jesus of Nazareth with the Holy Spirit and with power, who went about doing good and healing all who were oppressed by the devil, for God was with Him.
(Acts 10:38).

Whatever we think, Jesus healed them all. God does not have prejudices towards us; He does not value one person above another. Nor does He does show personal favouritism to any man, for there is no partiality with God, and what His word promises to do for one, is also a promise He will do for all.
Every single man and woman that God created, God loves equally.
For God so loved the world, His unconditional love is equal towards all of humanity.
(Galatians 2:6), (Romans 2:11), (Acts 10:34).

Though Gods love is unconditional towards us all, each of us has to deal with the problem of sin, for this has brought separation from God.
Mankind cannot save itself, we were born into a world of sin; inherited a sinful nature, therefore were sinners who had missed the mark, and fallen short of Gods standard.

Therefore, we needed a saviour.
(Romans 3:23, 6:23), (Ephesians 2:1-3), (Psalm 51:5).

The good news, which is the gospel, means that God does offer us salvation and eternal life through Jesus Christ.

God so loved the world that He gave His only begotten Son, that whoever believes in him should not perish but have everlasting life.
(John 3:16).

Today, anyone and everyone has the right and the opportunity to have all their sins forgiven and forgotten and inherit eternal life. The only requirement for us is to believe and receive. Jesus has taken our place, and paid the unimaginable price, so we are transformed through the miracle of new birth, into completely different people, new creations, not sinners but saints, no longer slaves to sin but Sons of God.
(Psalm 103:12), (John 1:13), (2 Corinthians 5:17), (Galatians 4:7), (Romans 10: 8-11).

The Father loves mankind, He does not give preference to one above another, and is long-suffering towards his creation, not wanting anyone to perish spiritually or physically, but everyone to come to repentance, *(2 Peter 3:9).*

I'm sure you have vivid memories of your childhood, for some it will be good, for others not good. For me, my Dad was my hero, he treated us as brothers and sisters the same. He only wanted the best for my life, and encouraged us to dream big and go for the destiny God had for each one of us. There were no favourites in our house, Dad's love and generosity was the same towards us all. This is just a glimpse of the love and the care which Father God has towards us all, from the smallest details in our lives to the greatest challenges in life, he is there with love and care, and is always planning for us. Whatever you are facing as a challenge in your life today, remember that God plans for you and his plans are good.

I know the plans I have for you declares the Lord, plans to prosper you and not to harm you, plans to give you hope and a future.
(Jeremiah 29:11).

God does not plan harm or destruction for us, if we are His children and called according to His purpose, He is working all things together for our good, *(Romans 8:28).* God has only good things mapped out for your life.
His plan was to send Jesus to the cross to become our substitute, and take our sin and diseases upon himself. For if He has paid the price for our sins to be forgiven, He has also paid the price for all sickness and disease to be healed today.

Through out this book, we will look to affirm and strengthen the facts, reality, and the consistency of scripture that God really does heal today.

Throughout the Bible, we find that God reveals Himself by His names. The names of God reveal a description of His personality, character, and nature. It identifies for us, what God is and what God does.

Kevin Conner says that to understand a name in Hebrew does not mean simply to be acquainted with it, but to have experience and history with the person to whom the name belongs.
Therefore, to know Gods name, is as much knowledge as it is experience. It gives us revelation of who He is and what He does, also it gives us an aspect of his personality and power that we can all be recipients of.

The name, 'Jehovah' occurs over 6823 times in the Old Testament, and it was His covenant name that He revealed to His people who knew Him more intimately, such as Abraham, who was called His friend.

Throughout history, God made covenant with His people, and simply put, a covenant was a binding agreement between two parties, the greater and the lesser. God obviously was the greater party and always made the initiative to make a covenant relationship with His people. With covenant, there were always conditions and there were always blessings, blessings for obedience and judgement for disobedience. *(Genesis 8:20-9:17), (Genesis 15), (Exodus 19), (Jeremiah 31:31-34).*

I have always seen covenant as much more than a contract or guarantee, because either one of those can have a time frame or an expiry date.
Today as believers, we are under a new covenant, a better covenant that has been paid for and established through the blood of Jesus.
(Hebrews 8:6).

It's eternal, unbreakable, whereby God vows to keep and be faithful to every promise He has made.
(Hebrews 13:20).

I am sure we have all, at one point in time, had a contract or a warranty with a company that promised an amazing guarantee, only to find over time it did not include everything you thought was promised. This happened with a car which my wife bought a few years ago. We were sold a warranty which we believed covered the suspension arm, only to find when the part broke, that it was not covered under the warranty.

I am glad that Gods cover and warranty is all inclusive for our lives. It's not a life time guarantee; it's an eternal one that has nothing left out. The covenant that God has with His people is one where all of His promises are yes and amen in Christ Jesus.
(2 Corinthians 1:20).

One of His covenant names that reveals His nature, will, and commitment to us is, Jehovah Rophe, which means the Lord who heals you.

If you diligently heed the voice of the Lord your God and do what is right in His sight, give ear to His commandments and keep all His statutes, I will put none of the diseases on you which I have brought on the Egyptians. For I am the Lord who heals you.
(Exodus 15:26).

This covenant name identifies a God who promises to heal you, it's what He naturally does and this is what He wants us to know and experience. In fact, from the above verse, it's clear that He did not want any of His people to know any type of diseases that the Egyptians knew. What was true then, is true today because Jehovah Rophe, is an eternal name of God, therefore if He healed Israel thousands of years ago, He will heal today because His name has not changed neither has His agreement with us.

I was reading, 'The Old Testament Healing Covenant' by Jack Hayford and he refers to *(Exodus 15:26)* and says, "This verse is widely referred to as the Old Testament Divine Healing Covenant. It is called a covenant, because in it God promises He will keep His people free from diseases and conditions the promise upon their diligent obedience. He goes on to say that the terms used for diseases and healing in the Hebrew indicate ailments of the body and their healing. This is not only a spiritual concept, but an intensely physical one."
His covenant promised to keep His people free from sickness, for Jehovah did not want His people living with pain and suffering.

"So you shall serve the Lord your God, and He will bless your bread and your water. And I will take sickness away from the

midst of you. No one shall suffer miscarriage or be barren in your land; I will fulfill the number of your days.
(Exodus 23: 25-26).

And the Lord will take away from you all sickness, and will afflict you with none of the terrible diseases of Egypt which you have known, but will lay them on all those who hate you.
(Deuteronomy 7:15).

What was true concerning Jehovah was also true concerning Jesus. His mission was to do only what He saw His Father doing. His purpose was not to do anything on his own initiative but to enforce the will of His Father, which was to heal and set free the captives.
(Luke 22:42), (John 5:19-20), (John 8:28).

When evening had come, they brought to Him many who were demon-possessed.
And He cast out the spirits with a word, and healed all who were sick.
(Matthew 8:16).

Jesus healed all that were sick, and was it His will? Yes, it was! He was willing to heal then, and He is willing to heal today.
At the beginning of *Matthew 8*, you find the story of a leper who comes to Jesus and says,

if you are willing you can make me clean, Jesus immediately says, I am willing be cleansed, and immediately his leprosy was cleansed.
(Matthew 8:2-3).

Jesus was willing with the leper and His will has not changed. I believe that He is willing to heal all sickness today. Don't doubt what His will is, His word and His promises are clear. The word of God has not changed; therefore the will of God has not changed.

Jesus is the same Yesterday, Today and Forever.
(Hebrews 13:8).

Don't have more faith in a Jesus of yesterday or a Jesus of tomorrow, than a Jesus of today. He is willing to heal you today. There are some Christians who believe that, for some mysterious reason or purpose, that God wants them sick, or God puts sickness on people to keep them humble, which is contrary to the nature of God. I believe that the scriptures unanimously teach us that we are to be healthy and whole.
In fact as we will discover, it's as easy for God to remove sickness and disease, as it is sin.

David celebrated this truth in *Psalm 103*, and declares that His will is to forgive all sin, and heal all your diseases. All is all, and He has left nothing out of the new covenant that we are now recipients of.

Praise the Lord, my soul;
all my inmost being, praise His holy name
Praise the Lord, my soul,
and forget not all His benefits—
who forgives all your sins
and heals all your diseases,
who redeems your life from the pit
and crowns you with love and compassion,
who satisfies your desires with good things
so that your youth is renewed like the eagle's.
(Psalm 103:1-5).

Chapter 2

Did Jesus Die for our Sickness and Diseases on the Cross?

This is a very important question, because if redemption for the whole man is not a part of the work of Christ dying on the cross, then we have no legal right and authority to believe for healing today. I believe that Jesus became our sacrifice and substitute on the Cross and took all sins and sicknesses upon Himself at Calvary. The last words of Jesus clarify and confirm this as He hung on the cross and uttered with His last breath, "IT IS FINISHED".
Through Christ's death He finished His work for humanity, and the price for our sin was paid in full.

Jesus was our Atonement, or in other words, He was our substitute, our scape goat. He took our place and paid the price, that we were rightfully guilty of and should have paid the penalty for. Under the Old Covenant, the problem of sin was dealt with by the sacrifice of animals which were either sheep, bulls or goats. They became the sin offering. They were sacrificed, and their blood was offered by priests for the sins of the people so that they could receive forgiveness. But nowhere in the Old Testament do you find animal sacrifice taking away sin. One of the Hebrew meanings for the word atonement means covered, therefore the sacrifice only

covered sin. This was a temporary, not perfect solution, which is why sacrifices had to be offered by the priests for the sins of the people time and time again.
(Leviticus 4:29-35, 8, 16).

The blood of animals was never meant to be a permanent sacrifice on behalf of God's people, because this method could never deliver us and free us from sin and death, they were only ever meant to be a substitute. Only Christ could come into this world to free us from the curse, for He was sinless and offered himself as a living sacrifice.

To cover sin is just like doing a spring clean in your home, you want to remove all the dirt out of the house and clean under every nook and cranny. However imagine if you constantly swept dirt underneath a rug or carpet; the dirt still remains in your home, we just can't see it anymore. The room looks clean but the dirt and the grime is just covered over.
The dirt has not been dealt with or moved out of reach, it is still under the rug. Jesus came so the dirt and grime and stain of sin could be removed and wiped away once and for all. He became sin so we could be free of sin. We have now been transferred or delivered out of the kingdom of darkness into the kingdom of His son. We are new creations, the old has passed again and all things have become new, and the blood of Jesus cleanses us from all sin.
(Colossians 1:13), (2 Corinthians 5:17), (2 Corinthians 5:21), (1 John 1:9).

But in those sacrifices there is a reminder of sins every year. For it is not possible that the blood of bulls and goats could take away sins.
(Hebrews 10:3-4).

Then He said, "Behold, I have come to do Your will, O God." He takes away the first that He may establish the second. By that will we have been sanctified through the offering of the body of Jesus Christ once for all.

And every priest stands ministering daily and offering repeatedly the same sacrifices, which can never take away sins. But this Man, after He had offered one sacrifice for sins forever, sat down at the right hand of God, from that time waiting till His enemies are made His footstool. For by one offering He has perfected forever those who are being sanctified.
(Hebrews 10:9-14).

We have received a great exchange that can only be described as sheer grace, for none of us deserved it? Our sins are not covered but taken away as far as the east is from the west.
(Psalm 103:12).

As Jesus achieved that for our sins, He also achieved it for all sickness and disease. Sin is the cause of sickness in our world today. It has its ultimate origin in sin because human suffering stems from the fall of Adam and Eve in the garden. *(Genesis 2:15-17), (Romans 1:20-32).*

Therefore, just as through one man sin entered the world, and death through sin, and thus death spread to all men, because all sinned.
(Romans 5:12).

When God created the earth in *(Genesis 1),* everything He made was good, man and woman who were made in his image, perfect and without sin. Mankind was created in God's image, without sin and sickness. When Adam and Eve rebelled against God, everything around and within us became fallen, and sin, sickness and death, entered the world. *(Genesis 3:1-19), (Romans 8:2), (Genesis 1:26-28).*

God is not the author of sickness, satan is. Jesus said, *"the thief comes to kill, steal and destroy, but I have come to give you life, and life in all its fullness."*
(John 10:10).

The mission and mandate of Jesus was to redeem us from the curse which had been placed on mankind. Redeem means to pay the price. His life was the price and by freely offering His life, He became the curse for us so that we could be freed from sin, sickness and disease.

Christ has redeemed us from the curse of the law, having become a curse for us for it is written, "Cursed is everyone who hangs on a tree."
(Galatians 3:13).

Jesus took the full measure of the curse that was meant for us, including the curses in *Deuteronomy 28* which are clearly physical, internal and mental; these verses mention sickness and disease.
(Deuteronomy 28:15-68).

He became that curse on the cross, so that we could be free from all the repercussions of the curse. Jesus body and blood became the payment, and it was finalised and finished over 2000 years ago. Every disease known to man, curable or incurable, past, present or future, was placed on the body of Christ, so that we could be free from our sins and free from all sickness.

Satan cannot legally lay on us, what God laid on Jesus. Christ became sick with our diseases that we might be healed. He knew no sickness until He became sick for us. The object of Christ's sin bearing was to make righteous all those who would believe in Him as their sin bearer. The object of His disease bearing was to make well all those who would believe in Him as their disease bearer. (Healing the Sick by T.L.Osborn).

Jesus was the only cure for the curse, and He settled the debt in full at the Cross, therefore if the price has been paid in full, then we have a legal right not only to have our sins forgiven, but also our sicknesses healed. God wants us to be well, and wants us fully convicted, and convinced concerning these truths.

The prophet Isaiah prophesied that healing is in the atonement for us, it's part of our inheritance that Jesus has bought through His sacrifice.

But He was wounded for our transgressions,
He was bruised for our iniquities;
The chastisement for our peace was upon Him,
And by His stripes we are healed.
(Isaiah 53:5).

In the gospel of Matthew, he records as an eye witness the life and ministry of Jesus. He states that all those who were demon possessed and sick were brought to Him, and He healed them all. He also referred to the words of Isaiah, and used them as His authority to heal. Jesus's life and ministry was a prophetic fulfilment and validation of the words of Isaiah. Healing the sick was confirmation of what Jesus was sent for, and was to die for.

When evening had come, they brought to Him many who were demon-possessed. And He cast out the spirits with a word, and healed all who were sick, that it might be fulfilled which was spoken by Isaiah the prophet, saying:
"He Himself took our infirmities
And bore our sicknesses."
(Matthew 8:16-17).

1 Peter, affirms again the truth, that Jesus took all of the sins and the sicknesses of the entire world at the Cross. He states that by His stripes we were healed. In other words, Jesus has already dealt with it, it's a done deal; Christ paid the price, by whose stripes you were healed. We are not waiting to know whether He will heal or not, healing was provided over Two Thousand years ago through the death, burial, and

resurrection of Jesus Christ, where He took sickness upon himself so that we can be healed.

Who Himself bore our sins in His own body on the tree, that we, having died to sins, might live for righteousness—by whose stripes you were healed.
(1 Peter 2:24).

Three times in scripture we are faced with the truth that Jesus took our infirmities, and bore our sicknesses, so that by His stripes we were healed. God's word reveals His will for us, it shows us that if Jesus has paid the price for our salvation, He paid the price for our healing, for when Jesus said it was finished, everything He gave his life for and died for was finished. We are qualified now, as children of God, to share in the inheritance that Christ has obtained for us. That inheritance includes healing.
(Colossians 1:12).

Our responsibility is to appropriate by faith what Christ has already done, and settle in our hearts that God will heal one and all today. We don't have to beg or plead but believe, receive and trust what the word of God promises to all believers, and according to His word we shall be healed.

Chapter 3

Does Healing Happen Today?

The answer to that question, is absolutely yes. In fact, as soon as Jesus established the New Covenant through His blood, and left this earth, the early church experienced and lived in the power of the Holy Spirit *(Acts 2)* and saw signs, wonders, and miracles happen before their very eyes.

We therefore see a transfer of the Holy Spirit from Jesus to the disciples after he ascends to heaven; this is evident in the life of the early church, because Jesus guarantee to them and to us is.

you shall receive power when the Holy Spirit comes upon us. (Acts 1:8).

Jesus's commission to His disciples and to us was to heal the sick.

And when He had called His twelve disciples to Him, He gave them power over unclean spirits, to cast them out, and to heal all kinds of sickness and all kinds of disease. (Matthew 10:1).

Heal the sick, cleanse the lepers, raise the dead, cast out demons. Freely you have received, freely give. (Matthew 10:8).

God is not a liar, *(Numbers 23:19)*, what He says He means. If He says He saves, He saves, if He says He heals, He heals,

God does not know what it is to lie, it's impossible and totally opposite to his character. Jesus also showed and demonstrated through His life that He wanted all people healed.

F.F. Bosworth once said, "Don't doubt God. If you must doubt something, doubt your doubts, because they are unreliable, but never doubt God, nor his word".

We can be free of disease and heal the sick because Jesus has given us as believers, power and authority over the devil, because Jesus came Into the world to destroy the works of the evil one.
(1 John 3:8).

Sickness is one of the works of the devil and Jesus has destroyed it. We are now qualified as believers to rule and reign in life, *(Romans 5:17)*, live like more than conquerors, (Romans 8:37), and enforce satan's defeat and celebrate Christ's victory. We are not trying to obtain power or authority; as we already have it.
(Mathew 16:18), (Luke 9: 1-2), (Luke 10:19).

Webster's Dictionary defines authority as the right to govern, control or command. It is delegated power from one at a higher level. From the youngest to the oldest believer, we have it, it's our inheritance and we should operate in it to bring Gods power and rulership into earthly situations. We might be in an ongoing war with the powers of darkness *(Eph 6:12),* but it's a war that's already won.

Inasmuch then as the children have partaken of flesh and blood, He Himself likewise shared in the same, that through death He might destroy him who had the power of death, that is, the devil.
(Hebrews 2:14).

Having disarmed principalities and powers, He made a public spectacle of them, triumphing over them in it. (Colossians 2:15).

Satan and his kingdom have been destroyed and he has been stripped and disarmed of all power, and we as Christians must enforce Christ victory and satan's defeat.

Nowhere in the life of the early church do we find anyone asking for healing and not being healed. In the book of Acts we find many records of healing.
(Acts 3:1-11), (5:12-15), (9:33-34), (9:36-41), (14:8-10), (16:16-18), (19:11-12).

Also a multitude gathered from the surrounding cities to Jerusalem, bringing sick people and those who were tormented by unclean spirits, and they were all healed. (Acts 5:16).

The believers in the book of Acts continued what Jesus began to do and teach, *(Acts1:1)*, enforcing Christ's victory they carried on with the work of the great physician and healed the sick. As all were healed in *(Acts 5:16)*, the God of love and compassion desires all to be healed today.
What they started we must continue now. For miracles and healing did not end with the early church, they are not extinct; they are very much alive and occurring in our twenty first century world.

I remember a number of years ago visiting my Grandfather for Sunday lunch. As we sat down to eat a meal together, my Grandfather started to have pain, and suddenly fell off his chair onto the floor unconscious, when we tried to find a pulse, there was none. Other family members started panicking and my Grandmother started to cry. The atmosphere seemed surreal as my Grandfather lay on the floor. Without thinking, I laid my hands on him and commanded all sickness and death to leave his body, and for God to restore him to health. Within a few minutes he sat up, completely unaware of anything that happened and completely healed.

The following week my Grandfather went to the doctors for a checkup and was told he was in better health than his last checkup, which was five years ago. This showed to me the nature of the God that we serve, He not only heals but He is also able to do exceedingly abundantly above all that we ask or think, *(Ephesians 3:20)*. God certainly did this for my Grandfather and He is able to do it for you.

We have the same connection with the promises and the power of God that Jesus and the early church had. The bible is as life changing and dynamic as it's always been, it's the only book on the planet that's living and active and sharper than any two edged sword *(Hebrews 4:12)*. Therefore God's word is His will that will always work in our lives.

Beloved, I pray that you may prosper in all things and be in health, just as your soul prospers. For I rejoiced greatly when brethren came and testified of the truth that is in you, just as you walk in the truth. I have no greater joy than to hear that my children walk in truth.
(3 John:2-4).

God wants you and me to know prosperity in all areas of life, and to be in health. The delight of this Apostolic Father was to know that his spiritual children, knew the truth, walked in it and experienced it for themselves.

In the New Testament one of the words commonly translated in the bible as saves or saved, is the word sozo,
(Mark 16:16), (Acts 2:21), (Romans 10:9). It is right that we use this word concerning salvation from sin, but it means much more than that.

In its fullest form it means to save, heal, restore, deliver and make whole. Therefore, the salvation that God offers is for the whole man, spirit, soul and body and we should settle for nothing less. It carries the meaning of physical and spiritual healing. When Jesus spoke to the leper in *(Luke 17:19)*, He said, "arise go on your way, your faith has made you whole" (sozo). Furthermore in *(Luke 8: 26-36)*, we find the story of Legion who was demon possessed, but through an encounter with Jesus, he who was possessed by demons was healed (sozo) verse 36. The word salvation (sozo) is an all-inclusive word, which offers full deliverance for us spiritually, physically and mentally. The writers of the New Testament showed the completeness of the word sozo by using it in different contexts to show us the full meaning of each aspect of salvation. Below are a few examples of the different characteristics of how sozo is used;

Salvation
"That if you confess with your mouth, 'Jesus is Lord,' and believe in your heart that God raised Him from the dead, you will be saved (sozo).
(Romans 10:9).

"For the Son of Man came to seek and to save (sozo) what was lost."
(Luke 19:10).

"For it is by grace you have been saved (sozo), through faith – and this not from yourselves, it is the gift of God."
(Ephesians 2:8).

Other scriptures: *(Acts 2:21), (Acts 2:47), (Acts4:12).*

Healing
"Jesus turned and saw her. 'Take heart, daughter,' he said, 'your faith has healed (sozo) you.' And the woman was healed (sozo) from that moment."
(Matthew 9:22).

"And wherever He went into villages, towns or countryside they placed the sick in the marketplaces. They begged Him to

let them touch even the edge of His cloak, and all who touched
Him were healed (sozo)."
(Mark 6:56).

Other scriptures: *(Mark 5:23), (Mark 10:52), (Acts 14:9).*

Deliverance

"Those who had seen it told the people how the demon-
possessed man had been cured (sozo).
(Luke 8:36).

"Jesus rebuked the demon, and it came out of the boy, and he
was healed (sozo) from that moment.
(Matthew 17:18).

Our salvation guarantee is internal and external and is all-inclusive, whether it's fear, mental illness, cancer, blindness, the emotional scars of sexual abuse, diabetes, or one of the tens of thousands of diseases in the world today, Jesus provided a full salvation that is complete and finished.
I can never understand how some Christians would believe that God will forgive and save us from our sins but not heal our bodies, that to me does not make sense. God's original design for mankind was to be made in God's image, according to their likeness *(Genesis 1:26)*, that's perfect without sin or sickness. What was lost through the first Adam has been restored through the second Adam, Jesus.
(1 Corinthians 15:45).

I often think back to a time when my wife had a major abscess in her mouth and the pain was unbearable. At the time, she had not experienced the healing power of God, nor was she saved, and I was not in a right relationship with Jesus. She had tried alcohol, and pain killers to numb the pain and still it was getting worse. It was the middle of the night and no dentist was available. I said to her that I had tried everything except pray for her; she said, "What good will that do?" So I briefly explained that you can pray for people and they can get healed, so she agreed.

To be honest, I had no faith, no hope and no expectation, I laid my hand on her mouth, said a few words and Jesus immediately healed her, which she could not believe. That had nothing to do with me, but everything to do with God's grace. That experience taught me a lesson.

God wants to heal people any time of the day or the night, and is more eager and willing to do it than we are to pray, or at times even believe.

God is full of compassion and mercy, and just like Jesus was moved with compassion and healed the sick, *(Matthew 14:14)*, so He continually desires to demonstrate his compassion and power on the needy today.

Chapter 4

Agape Love the Key Ingredient.

Study the bible and one of the first truths that captures our attention is that God is love, it's who He is, and characterises everything He does. Probably the most famous verse in the bible is *(John 3:16)*, which says, *"For God so loved the world that He gave,"* then *(1 John 3:16)*, says this, *"by this we know love; because he laid down His life for us."*

God the father gave His Son, and the Son laid down His life for us, His love was giving, His love was sacrificial. Love describes the very being of God, love is who He is, God is love, *(1 John 4:8, 16)*.

Love defines His character; every action He takes is motivated by love, for God holds the well-being of others as His primary concern. He is not trying to love, He is love and that's what He automatically does.

We are here today because of that life giving unconditional love. We have not just heard about that, no, we have known that love, experienced it, and been immersed in its life changing power.

Love in the English language is difficult to define, because all we have is one word. For example, I love my wife, and of course she loves me, I love to read, and she loves our dog, Dylan. We, of course, have different degrees to what we love the most, but it's hard sometimes to describe, or characterise the difference, when in the English language we only have one word, and it reads the same.

In the Greek you have a number of different words for love, the greatest and most profound is the word Agape.

Agape is the God kind of love found in the New Testament, and it's unconditional, sacrificial, selfless love, not just words but it's like a verb; it's a doing word. If it says something, it does it. It's motivated by action; it's less affection, more a decision, less a feeling, more an action.

It's Gods deliberate choice to do something without a logical cause. There was no logical reason, why God would ever love you or me, you will never work it out. In fact, the opposite was true. *(Ephesians 2:1)* says, we were dead in our trespasses and sins!

God is not attracted to sin, in fact He is repulsed by sin, He hates it, and we were dead in our sins, yet God made a choice to love us, and to give His son for us.

God wasn't attracted to you and didn't choose you because you were big and important—the fact is, there was almost nothing to you. He did it out of sheer love, keeping the promise He made to your ancestors.
(Deuteronomy 7:7-10 MSG).

Watch what God does, and then you do it, like children who learn proper behaviour from their parents. Mostly what God does is love you. Keep company with Him and learn a life of love. Observe how Christ loved us.
His love was not cautious but extravagant. He didn't love in order to get something from us but to give everything of Himself to us. Love like that.
(Ephesians 5:1-2 MSG)

That line sums up Agape love. He didn't love in order to get something from us, but to give everything of Himself to us, that's unthinkable, unexplainable, but that's the Agape love of God, not cautious but extravagant.

Paul states in *1 Corinthians 13* that, the greatest is love, there is nothing greater, or nothing more supreme than this God given quality, and that is the foundation and the motivation for everything God does, including healing. He heals us because he loves us.

Then they cried out to the Lord in their trouble,
And He saved them from their distresses.
He sent His word and healed them,
And rescued them from their destruction.
Let them give thanks to the Lord for His loving kindness,
And for His wonderful acts to the children of men!
(Psalm 107:17).

Because of God's loving kindness, He heard their cry, saved them from their distresses, sent His word and healed them. A God of loving kindness was the answer then, and He's the answer for all sickness and disease today. Whether we are in need of healing or are praying for the sick, we must ensure that love has the foremost place, for this is firstly the reason He heals, He overwhelmingly and extravagantly loves people, and when healing is administrated through love, love never fails.
(1 Corinthians 13:8).

In the gospel's we find that Jesus demonstrated His power not just to prove that He was God, but also to show that He was God abounding in love and compassion, that was His motivation for healing and deliverance, His compassion turned into action.

The word compassion means to suffer with someone, the definition of compassion is, "a feeling of deep sympathy or

sorrow for another who is stricken with misfortune, accompanied by the strong desire to alleviate the suffering."
True compassion moved Jesus to do something for others.
Compassion was more than a passing feeling, for Jesus felt the sufferings of others from the depth of his being, which then became his motivation to change their situation.

Then Jesus went about all the cities and villages, teaching in their synagogues, preaching the gospel of the kingdom, and healing every sickness and every disease among the people. But when He saw the multitudes, He was moved with compassion for them, because they were weary and scattered, like sheep having no shepherd.
(Matthew 9:36-36).

And when Jesus went out He saw a great multitude; and He was moved with compassion for them, and healed their sick.
(Matthew 14:14).

Whatever you are facing today, the Lord is still gracious and full of compassion towards you.
(Psalm 145:8).

He is not against you, He is for you.
He was moved with compassion for the multitude in Jesus' day, so He is moved and ready to demonstrate his love and compassion towards you right now.

I remember when I was working as a salesman, and every Friday would be the day I went into the office. On one occasion I was sat at my desk, and started talking to the sales person next to me. I was new in the job, but as we were talking, I felt an intense sense of God's love and mercy for this man. It was a very uncommon feeling, but very strong.
I told him I was a Christian and asked if I could pray for him and he said yes. As I prayed, I felt an overwhelming sense of the compassion of Jesus, and I sensed he had a major problem with his back.

I therefore commanded all pain to leave his back, immediately he fell to the floor, which was an interesting dilemma in the office. A few minutes later he told me he had a severe back problem for a number of years, but was now pain free, and could bend down perfectly.

What I felt at that moment, was what God feels concerning mankind all the time. He constantly feels love, and mercy and compassion towards His creation. He is not immune, or isolated from what we feel, our High Priest Jesus is touched with the feeling of our infirmities, *(Hebrews 4:15)*, He feels what we feel, and understands our condition but through the cross has freed us from all our enemies, because His love endures forever.
(Psalm 136:24).

Sickness and disease is an enemy of God, Jesus defeated them at the Cross, through His everlasting love. They have no authority over or rightful place in the life of the believer. God wants you well, even if you have been sick for many years, trust Him again, and watch Him perform a miracle in your life.

David declared the will of God in Psalm 34.

Many are the afflictions of the righteous,
But the Lord delivers him out of them all.
(Psalm 34:19).

The International Standard Bible Encyclopaedia states that the word affliction in *(Psalm 34:19)* means, misery, injury, trouble, mental distress, bodily pain, sickness, poverty, oppression etc.

You might be facing many afflictions today, but as a Christian you are righteous, *(2 Corinthians 5:21)*, *(Romans 5:1)*, and God promises to deliver you not from some, but from all afflictions.

All we have to do is believe in His word more than our circumstances. God's word reveals here again that healing and deliverance is His will, not sometimes but all the time, and we have to be more convinced in what the word says than what the doctors or our condition says.

Chapter 5

The Medicine of the Word.

There is life changing power in the word of God. The bible is more than a good book, or a great novel, Its God's word, *(1 John 1:1)*, God breathed, *(2 Timothy 3:16)*, living and active, *(Hebrew 4:16)*, supernatural in origin, we have everything if we have His word.

His divine power has given us everything we need for a godly life through our knowledge of him who called us by His own glory and goodness.
(2 Peter 1:3).

That divine power is the word, *(Hebrews 1:3)*, and everything in existence is held together by the word of His power. His word is settled in Heaven, *(Psalm 119:89)*, we are to live by His word, *(Mathew 4:4)*, so we can enjoy a victorious godly life. Now, to access and live in the fullness of the power of His word takes a requirement and a responsibility from us.

Praise God for the promise, everything means everything, He's left nothing out, that's why all the promises of God are yes and amen to you today in Christ Jesus, *(2 Corinthians 1:20)*, but the requirement for us is to find out and know what those promises are, and that happens when we put the word first place in our lives.

Determine today to give the word of God priority in your life, make a quality decision to read it and meditate on it, instead of it gathering dust all week on the coffee table. The supernatural

change in your life will amaze you. When you open the bible, you are reading a life changing book, that brings with it, not information but transformation.
(Hebrews 4:12).

I remember preaching in a church a number of years ago concerning the importance of the word of God. I asked the congregation of around 180 people, how many had read their bible once in the last week. Less than 25 raised their hands. In a statistic by Barna group, four in ten adults said they did not have time to read the bible, in another survey only 13 percent said they had time to read the bible daily. Unfortunately, this has become the state of the Twenty First century church, we have become lazy, secularised and too busy for a life changing God. This has to change.

"Whatever keeps me from my bible is my enemy, however harmless it may appear to be." A W Tozer.

One of the greatest enemies to spiritual breakthrough is a lack of knowledge.

My people are destroyed for lack of knowledge.
(Hosea 4:6).

To know the will of God concerning healing we cannot be complacent, we must understand the word of God and take time to read it and meditate on it for ourselves, and apply it and personalise it to our lives, because as we do, healing and wholeness are promised.

He sent His word and healed them, and delivered them from their destructions.
(Psalm 107:20).

My son, pay attention to what I say; turn your ear to my words.
Do not let them out of your sight; keep them within your heart;

for they are life to those who find them and health to one's
whole body.
(Proverbs 4:20-22).

The word of God is like medicine. In fact, the word for health here is the Hebrew word for medicine. Just like you and I would take tablets or a prescription from the doctor for any illness in our body, so the word of God is the prescription or medicine we have to take every day, for as we give our attention to it and get our heart full of it, it will be health to our whole body. The key to your miracle today is the word of God, what you hold in your hands has the power to deliver you.

Keys to unlocking the words healing power

God's word has to live in us
Scripture teaches that we have been born again not of corruptible seed, but of incorruptible, by the word of God which lives and abides forever, *(1 Peter 1:23)*. The word of God is divine seed, its spiritual food for the inner man, you feed on the seed truths in the word of God, and it will change you from the inside out and produce a harvest in your life.
When the seed of God's word starts to expand and germinate within you, it will demolish spiritual strongholds and tear down wrong thinking, and cause you to live from Gods perspective.
It might take time and diligence to feed on the seed of God's word, and meditate on it day and night, *(Joshua 1:8-9)*, but God cannot be mocked, what we sow we shall reap. *(Galatians 6:7).*

Then Jesus said to those Jews who believed Him, "If you
abide in My word, you are My disciples indeed. And you shall
know the truth, and the truth shall make you free."
(John 8:31-32).

I have heard many Christians quote verse 32 and say, when we know the truth, the truth shall make or set you free, but the condition is verse 31 which says that we must abide in his word. As we abide or live in his word, or as one commentator states, make the word our daily home, we will know the truth, and the truth of God's word will sets us free.

Jesus also said, if you abide in me, and my words abide in you, you will ask what you desire, and it shall be done for you.
(John 15:7).

One version says ask anything and it shall be done for you. When we are full of the word, and place Jesus first, everything is possible, all we have to do is ask.

I recently heard a testimony, of a lady diagnosed with MS at twenty eight years of age. Her condition worsened to the point where she needed crutches to walk. One day after hearing her pastor speak about the power of God's word and Jesus being the same yesterday today and forever, she started to have an expectancy for healing. She started to meditate and give attention to the word daily. After a few months, she started to feel slowly and slightly better. One evening she went to bed and dreamed that she was being plugged into a battery charger. As she awoke in the morning, she was completely healed. The truth and medicine of the word, set this lady free, and the truth of the word can set you free and heal and release you without anyone laying their hands on you.

God's word is living and active and sharper than any two edged sword.
(Hebrews 4:12).

Therefore, when we read it we are tapping into a life changing power that has greater power than any disease in your body right now. Realise today that the word has the final say on any trial, tribulation or illness we are experiencing at this moment. God's word is settled in heaven.

It has final authority.
(Psalm 119:89).

God and his word are one.
(John 1:1).

He is watching over his word to perform it.
(Jeremiah 1:12).

His word is sent to heal us.
(Psalm 107:20).

God has done His part, He has given it to us as a God breathed, God inspired legal document, for when the word speaks, God speaks, therefore, we have to act and sow the seed and plant the promises of God in our hearts until they release their life-giving power into our physical bodies and healing comes.

The Force of Faith
Faith is the fruit of the word, as we meditate on it, the word supernaturally creates faith, it's the by product of a life abiding in the word, that's the source of faith, if we are students of the word we will be a people of faith.
The bible is very clear concerning how faith is conceived.

So then faith comes by hearing, and hearing by the word of God.
(Romans 10:17).

The Greek meaning for word in this verse is the word Rhema, faith comes by hearing the Rhema word of God. This is the now word of God, the quickened word, that makes you alive on the inside. As we read His word, the Holy Spirit gives us revelation on what we have read.
Revelation is a heavenly truth that you could never know by the natural mind. It's like being in a room filled with darkness, unable to move forward or do anything because all you see is

darkness. When someone then turns the light on, your eyes are opened and you see everything that's visible and available to you. You also have freedom of movement, or can leave the room because your sight is restored and you see the detail. Revelation is like that, it brings light and clarity to a darkened and uninformed mind, therefore, diligence to the word, brings revelation not information and then faith comes.

As the people of God we are called to live by faith.
Faith is our anchor into the unseen realm, it becomes the evidence in our hearts of heavenly realities that are unseen. *(Hebrews 11:1).*

Faith pulls the promises of God from the unseen realm into our natural world so that the miraculous can happen.

We walk by faith not by sight .
(2 Corinthians 5:7).

So many live this verse in reverse order, they live by sight; they live dominated by their physical senses and the visible world rather than the spiritual. God is a rewarder of faith, and without faith it is impossible to please Him, *(Hebrews 11:6),* therefore to receive from God we have to believe that He will do what He says He will do.

"Faith sees the invisible, believes the unbelievable, and receives the impossible."
Corrie Ten Boom.

The blind
And when He had come into the house, the blind men came to Him. And Jesus said to them, "Do you believe that I am able to do this?" They said to Him, "Yes, Lord." Then He touched their eyes, saying, "According to your faith let it be to you." And their eyes were opened.
(Matthew 9:28-30).

The woman with the issue of blood

When she heard about Jesus, she came behind Him in the crowd and touched His garment. For she said, "If only I may touch His clothes, I shall be made well."
Immediately the fountain of her blood was dried up, and she felt in her body that she was healed of the affliction. And Jesus, immediately knowing in Himself that power had gone out of Him, turned around in the crowd and said, "Who touched My clothes?" But His disciples said to Him, "You see the multitude thronging You, and You say, 'Who touched Me?'" And He looked around to see her who had done this thing. But the woman, fearing and trembling, knowing what had happened to her, came and fell down before Him and told Him the whole truth. And He said to her, "Daughter, your faith has made you well. Go in peace, and be healed of your affliction."
(Mark 5:27-34).

The crippled

And in Lystra a certain man without strength in his feet was sitting, a cripple from his mother's womb, who had never walked. This man heard Paul speaking. Paul, observing him intently and seeing that he had faith to be healed, said with a loud voice, "Stand up straight on your feet!" And he leaped and walked.
(Acts 14:8).

All it took in these scriptures above was faith; release your faith in a God who heals today.
You might feel you have faith as small as a mustard seed, but it can and it will still move your mountain, *(Mark 11:22-24)*. Apparently, a mustard seed in biblical times was a seed that could hardly be seen by the naked eye. It was one of the smallest seeds. Your faith might be like that, it might seem small, but it's not insignificant.
Like the sick mentioned in the stories we have read, have faith in God, don't doubt in your heart what God promises to do, He is ready and willing to heal all your diseases.
(Psalm 103:3).

Stand on the word in faith, believe in your heart, pray to God in faith, and the answer is guaranteed.

And the prayer of faith will save the sick, and the Lord will raise him up.
(James 5:15).

A few years ago, when we lived in Bradford, my wife, Anna was involved in 3 car crashes within 3 months (these were all uninsured drivers). This left her with terrible back and neck pain and a trapped nerve in her neck.
After three separate physiotherapy courses failed to do anything, acupuncture also failed and the pain medication just sedating rather than killing the pain, she was forced to leave work. The doctors didn't seem to be able to do much in way of healing her, it was more medicating her.
One day when she was driving around a roundabout to pick the children up from school, she heard clearly the words of her friend, ringing in her ears, saying, sometimes you have to stand in faith and believe for things like healing even if you don't see any difference.

You see, Anna had heard this said many times before, but this time it was revelation. So from that moment on, she said to herself no matter how bad the pain was, she would make her confession the same as the bible, by His stripes we are healed. When I came home that evening from work, she told me that she had no pain anymore, which was wonderful I thought. She later told me that it took her three weeks to feel any difference, in her body, but day by day she got stronger and fitter and was able to lead a normal, pain free life again.

Confession brings possession
Words are important; with our words we either agree with God, or disagree with Him.
They will either be filled with faith, or fear, and will believe either God's truth or the devil's lies.

God's word released through your lips creates a miracle through your mouth. When we line up our confession with God's will, our words become a creative force that will change and transform our world.

In *Hebrews 11:3*, it says that the world was framed by the word of God, out of nothing God created something, the heavens and the earth.
Numerous times in Genesis 1, God said, and it was, so nothing was created without God speaking it into being.
We are created in the imago of God, *(Genesis 1:26-28)*, in His likeness, therefore our words carry power, what we sow with our words will eventually create a harvest in our lives.

If you confess with your mouth that Jesus is Lord and believe in your heart that God raised him from the dead, you will be saved.
(Romans 10:9).

Saved is the word sozo, (save, heal, restore, deliver and make whole). Believing and confessing brings wholeness to the total man.

Confession is affirming something which you believe, it is testifying of something that you know, it is witnessing of a truth which you embrace. Confession is repeating with our lips what God has said in His word. I'm not saying that we repeat words like robots, that would mean they would be empty and have no meaning. We speak the word from a place of understanding, and therefore defeat every enemy that stands against us.

And they overcame him by the blood of the Lamb and by the word of their testimony, and they did not love their lives to the death.
(Revelation 12:11).

We overcome the enemy by the word of our testimony, the power of our confession, just like Jesus did. Every time the

devil came to tempt Jesus, He did not remain silent. No, the authority of His speech was the word, for His answer to satan was, it is written, it is written, it is written.
We must also choose to speak the right words over our lives.

Death and life are in the power of the tongue, and those who love it will eat its fruit.
(Proverbs 18:21).

There is power in the tongue, it will produce death or life, the choice is yours. There used to be a nursery rhyme that I knew as a child which said, sticks and stones may break my bones, but names will never hurt me. This is certainly not true, because bones can heal, but evil words spoken to you, maybe when you were a child at an impressionable age, can keep you in an internal prison for the rest of your life. Words can hurt, they can destroy people, that's why our speech must be Godly, we must tame our tongue, because if we can, we will experience God's perfection in our life.

Our speech sets the course of our lives.
(James 3:1-10).

Out of the abundance of the heart the mouth speaks.
(Matthew 12:34).

In other words, what you fill your inner world with, your mind and your soul, will eventually come out of your mouth. That's why God's word needs to dwell within us richly, *(Colossians 3:16)*, for when you are full of the word, and suddenly the crises, or disaster walks into your life, the word comes out.

A number of years ago, I began to blame myself for not being a good father to my children. There were a number of circumstances, including divorce, that separated me from my children. They came through the trauma exceptionally well, but my heart became sick. I allowed myself to listen to the lies of the enemy and the words of critical people, and allowed guilt and condemnation to rule this area of my life. I was sick internally, which is as real as being sick physically. One day I went to a friend's house, who knew nothing concerning what I was going through. He made me a cup of coffee, and as he brought it to me, he said God told me to give you this cup with this logo on. It said, "The Worlds Number 1 DAD." As I saw and heard what he said, I broke down and cried and the healing process begun.

That was the beginning, and the attacks from the enemy and people still came. However as I meditated on God's word, and saw who I was from His perspective, and confessed His word, and challenged anyone who said I was a poor father, by saying, "no I am a great father". God says I'm a number one father, within a few months I was totally free. You see, I changed my perspective, I started to think differently and I started to speak differently. My words began the healing process because words heal.

The words of the reckless pierce like swords, but the tongue of the wise brings healing.
(Proverbs 12:18).

The tongue that heals is a tree of life, but a devious tongue breaks the spirit.
(Proverbs 15:4).

Speaking is part of the process that brings healing.
The woman with the issue of blood, received her healing by faith and also by her confession.

For she had been saying to herself, "If I only touch His outer robe, I will be healed.
(Matthew 9:21).

Start speaking today, what God says about you; begin to declare His, healing promises over your life. Don't speak fear, speak faith. Don't speak doubt, speak belief.

Chapter 6

How God Heals.

How and when God heals is a very important question that we must take time to discover, concerning the subject of healing. God heals today, His name Jehovah Rapha declares, I am the Lord who heals you, His name is a self-revelation of who He is and what He does. His will is to heal, yet the outworking of the healing miracle could be different from one person to the next.

I remember hearing A.A. Allan say before he prayed for a lame man, "God's the healer, I'm the believer." God heals, and we believe, how He sovereignly outworks the miracle though is down to Him, the only requirement for us is to believe.

God does and can heal instantly; we see this in the life and ministry of Jesus.

Blind Bartmaeus
Then Jesus said to him, "Go your way; your faith has made you well." And immediately he received his sight and followed Jesus on the road.
(Mark 10:52).

The Leper
Then He put out His hand and touched him, saying, "I am willing; be cleansed." Immediately the leprosy left him.
(Luke 5:13).

I have seen instant healing in our own families lives. On one occasion, our daughter had verruca's on both her feet. The soles of her feet were completely covered and it was very painful for her to walk. My wife and I prayed before bed one night, and when she woke up the next morning, there were no verruca's on her feet, just the holes where the infection had fallen out, Jesus can and still heals instantly today.

Healing can also be progressive; this sometimes can be hard to understand as I'm sure all of us would desire an instantaneous touch from God.

"For My thoughts are not your thoughts, Nor are your ways My ways," says the Lord. "For as the heavens are higher than the earth, So are My ways higher than your ways, and My thoughts than your thoughts.
(Isaiah 55:8-9).

God's ways and thoughts are higher than ours, they are different to ours, He sees the end from the beginning, and sometimes it does not make sense why we have to wait and stand on the word and believe for a period of time until the breakthrough comes, but it will come.
I have prayed for people in healing lines and seen one person instantaneously healed, and the next person leave without any apparent healing, but still believing God for the manifestation of the miracle. This to me is a mystery, but every time I pray for someone, my faith and prayer is that the power of God would heal them instantaneously.

I am still praying for the day that Smith Wigglesworth prophesied about before his death, when he said there will be a day before the return of Jesus, when everyone who encounters a Spirit filled believer shall be healed. That's my goal; that's my vision. His ways might be different to ours, but His will is to heal.

In the ministry of Jesus we see two accounts of progressive healing.

Then He came to Bethsaida; and they brought a blind man to Him, and begged Him to touch him.
So He took the blind man by the hand and led him out of the town.
And when He had spit on his eyes and put His hands on him, He asked him if he saw anything.
And he looked up and said, "I see men like trees, walking."
Then He put His hands on his eyes again and made him look up. And he was restored and saw everyone clearly.
(Mark 8:22-25).

Jesus here, prayed twice for the blind man, as it was clear that in the first instance, the man had only received a partial healing. This is the only instance in the gospels where Jesus lays hands on a person and prays twice, and it shows us that God can either heal instantly or in progressive stages.

Another instance we find in the gospels is the story of the ten lepers.

And they lifted up their voices and said, "Jesus, Master, have mercy on us!"
So when He saw them, He said to them, "Go, show yourselves to the priests." And so it was that as they went, they were cleansed.
(Luke 17:13-14).

It's interesting to note in these verses that it was as they went they were healed, as they left the presence of Jesus, and did what Jesus told them to do in obedience, which was to go show yourselves to the priests.
As they left His presence and went in obedience, obeying His words in the direction of the temple, they were healed. Again, there was a process of time here between, Jesus word and the manifestation of healing.
We also find another promise of Jesus, given to us as believers, concerning laying our hands on the sick.

In Luke 4 it says that, all those who had any that were sick, with various diseases brought them to Him, and He laid His hands on every one of them, and healed them.
This is one way which Jesus healed then, through his hands and also today, He does it through our hands.

And these signs will follow those who believe: In My name they will cast out demons; they will speak with new tongues; they will take up serpents; and if they drink anything deadly, it will by no means hurt them; they will lay hands on the sick, and they will recover."
(Mark 16:17-18).

These signs follow believers, therefore as Christians we are called to preach the gospel, cast out demons and heal the sick through the laying on of our hands. When you look carefully at *(Mark 16:18),* the word there is recover.

Rick Renner gives this commentary on this verse:
"When you look carefully at Mark 16:18 you'll notice that Jesus promised recovery. That recovery could be instantaneous, or it could be a process that is prolonged over a period of time. The complete Greek phrase here, could be translated, they shall progressively feel themselves getting better and better, until they are well and healthy. This lets us know that all healing does not happen instantly, some of them happen over a period of time. Just as medicine slowly works to reverse a medical condition, the power of God that was deposited with the laying on of our hands will begin to attack the work of the devil and progressively bring that sick person back into a state of health and wellbeing."
Sparkling gems from the Greek page 487 & 488.

Since 2008, my Father, John Edwards, has been ill and diagnosed as being diabetic and having Alzheimer's disease. Over the last five years he has progressively become worse and naturally, the symptoms seemed a greater reality than the promises of God. But during this time, I and my wife have never seen these sicknesses as something that belonged to my Father, or something that he should emotionally or verbally own. We have never said or inferred that they were John's sickness, no, we have seen them as a demonic enemy that was attacking a man of God. We have continually sought to encourage and strengthen my Mother, that Jesus was the healer who paid for and legally took this sickness upon his body over two thousand years ago.

As a family, in the face of an emotional and mentally tasking trial, we have tried to stand on the word, confess the power of the word and believe for the day of breakthrough. Earlier this year my Father went back to the doctor, and the doctor said he was no longer diabetic. For this, we give God the praise.
Personally, I see this as the first stage of his healing, and as often as I can, I pray and thank God for his healing. Would I have preferred for my Father not to have gone through this trial? Yes. Can I understand why God allowed it to happen. No. But my position is to trust, not to question, and to realise it's been sent by an enemy.

Jesus said in *(John 16:33)*, in this world you will have tribulation, but be of good cheer, I have overcome the world. He has overcome the world, therefore we can overcome anything we face in life, that's why the bible calls us to overcome.
(Revelation 2:7 - 3:21).

Now every time I see my Dad, I lay hands on him and declare that he will fully recover, because Jesus is the victor over all sickness and disease. I will never change my position on that, until I see my Father fully restored.

Jesus was never sympathetic concerning sickness and disease, He never saw it as a teacher He saw it as His enemy.

With the man bound with the evil spirit in Mark 1, and Simon's wife's mother, who was sick with a high fever, He rebuked the spirit and the sickness and immediately they were both healed and whole. Jesus never negotiated with the enemy. He never had pity on sickness, He released righteous, holy anger to destroy the enemies work, and so must we. *(Mark 1:21-28), (Mark 1:29-31).*

For this purpose the Son of God, was manifest, that he might destroy the works of the evil one.
(1 John 3:8).

I understand that it can get very tiring and draining, particularly when you live with pain and suffering. Nobody knows what it's like to walk in the shoes of another, who might have been sick for most of their lives. But may I encourage you today, don't give up, don't accept your circumstances as the final outcome concerning your future, start meditating on the promises of God.

Keep believing and keep asking. Don't accept this intruder, this infirmity, as your lot in life. God is bigger than your sickness and the word you hold in your hands, He has exalted above His name, *(Psalm 138:2).* One version says He has magnified His word above His name, magnified means that He's made it bigger. His word is His priority for your circumstance, and He is watching over His word to perform it. *(Jeremiah 1:12).*

Let's learn to be like the persistent widow woman whom Jesus spoke about in a parable in Luke 18. He speaks about always praying and not giving up. The widow woman demanded justice from an adversary, and she came before an unjust judge, persistently and continually asking for justice until he avenged her. God is not unjust, He's just, and Jesus finishes by giving the explanation to the story.

And shall God not avenge His own elect who cry out day and night to Him, though He bears long with them? I tell you that He will avenge them speedily.
(Luke 18:7-8).

Let's make a demand on God, and a demand on His promises. There might be a time frame between the promise and the provision, but as we cry out to Him day and night, He promises to answer speedily.
Sometimes we complain, or we moan to others and to God about our circumstances in life, but never speak to God about them. It's time to go to the source and ask.

You do not have because you do not ask.
(James 4:2).

Let's get bold in our asking because we know His will, let's not allow fear, or lies from the enemy, or failure to trust God in the past stop us from making a fresh demand on His word today. We have this confidence, that if we ask anything concerning His will, He hears us. This is not a time to give up, or grow weary, but to be persistent, because if we don't give up God promises that we will reap a harvest.

And since we know He hears us when we make our requests, we also know that He will give us what we ask for.
(1 John5:15).

Ask and keep on asking and it will be given to you; seek and keep on seeking and you will find; knock and keep on knocking and the door will be opened to you. For everyone who keeps on asking receives, and he who keeps on seeking finds, and to him who keeps on knocking, it will be opened.
(Mathew 7:7-8 Amplified).

Chapter 7

Partnering with the Holy Spirit.

The Holy Spirit is our teacher; in fact, Jesus told us that:

However, when he, the Spirit of Truth, has come, he will guide you into all Truth.
(John 16:13).

If we want freedom from addiction, bondage, or infirmities we must find a fresh dependancy on the Spirit, for without Him we cannot experience transformation. When His presence is present, immediately the power of God is available to heal. *(Luke 5:17).*

As Christians, the Holy Spirit now lives within us. Our bodies are now a temple that the Holy Spirit lives within.

Or do you not know that your body is the temple of the Holy Spirit who is in you, whom you have from God, and you are not your own?
(1 Corinthians 6:19).

And I will pray the Father, and he will give you another Helper, that he may abide with you forever.
(John 14:16).

The truths in these verse's can change your life forever, because the Spirit of God has not come to live on a temporary basis, He lives in us permanently. We are anointed with the Holy Spirit, *(1 John 2:20)*. His anointing upon and in our lives has the power to break every yoke of bondage. *(Isaiah 10:27)*.

I believe our bodies that are the temple of God, where designed by God, to live and be in health. God, who lives within us, does not know sickness, so why should our soul or body settle for anything less? There is no sickness in God or in heaven, and our prayer should be, Lord as it is in heaven let it be on earth, for if you are living in me let there be no sickness in my body.

We are now anointed by the Holy Spirit to heal the sick, and release the bound and the oppressed, *(Luke 4:18-19), (1 John 2:20,27)*. If the anointing within us and upon us can bring healing to others, surely it can bring health to our own bodies.

We are created in his image and likeness, *(Genesis 1:26-27)*, and our identity is now In Christ, In Him, we live and move and have our being. We never leave this place of living and thriving in Him, that's why, corporately, we are called the body of Christ.
We are Jesus to our world, that's why, it says;

As He is so are we in this world.
(1 John 4:17).

We are to be like Christ in this world. When Jesus lived and walked the earth, He never knew sickness or disease, He lived healthy, sickness could not touch Him. Therefore, why should we settle for anything else today, in our own lives?

God anointed Jesus of Nazareth with the Holy Spirit and with power, who went around doing good and healing all who were oppressed by the devil, for God was with Him.
(Acts 10:38).

What Jesus did in others, He can do in us today. For the same anointing and power that was on Him rests and remains upon us, and has the power to heal us from all oppression, depression, bondage, and assault of the enemy.

We must allow the Holy Spirit to help us break free from anything and everything that keeps us living according to natural conditions, rather than our position in Christ, for we live from our position not our condition. The nature of the Holy Spirit is to heal, in fact when His presence was manifest in the ministry of Jesus, it was said;

His power was present to heal, and all were healed.
(Luke 5:17).

Even amongst the gifts of the Spirit in *1 Corinthians 12*, we have the gifts of healing's and the working of miracles. Both are expressions of his character and nature, which He wants to manifest to profit and benefit us all.

To grow in our understanding, and experience of the Holy Spirit, we must understand the following.

Dependancy & Intimacy

Jesus was totally dependant on The Holy Spirit, He did not enter into ministry, teach, heal or do any mighty miracle until he received the fullness of the Holy Spirit, and then He walked in the power of the Spirit.
Just like Jesus, we must be dependant on the Holy Spirit, and invite and surrender every area of our lives to Him. He is God on the inside of you, your friend, your senior partner. Develop an intimate daily relationship with him, today.

Continual Filling

God wants you continually full of the Holy Spirit. You were not created to be full of this world, but full of God.

And do not be drunk with wine, in which is dissipation; but be filled with the Spirit. The Greek word for filled here is to be continually filled, meaning God never wants you empty of Holy Spirit; you can live full all the time.
(Ephesians 5:8).

He leads you to the word.

The word and the Spirit working together in your life can, and will, bring transformation to anything you are facing today. *Ephesians 6* says, that the sword of the Spirit is the word of God. The word and the Spirit are an eternal sword which can demolish and cut away anything that's contrary to Gods will for you. When you read the word, dependent on the Holy Spirit, He will open your eyes, and give you revelation.

Chapter 8

Hindrances to Healing.

Since it is clear in scripture that God is willing to heal, we still need to ask the question, why are so many Christians sick?
Are there hindrances or blockages that stop the flow of God's healing power?
Does God make requirements of us, and are there conditions that we must fulfil?
This chapter seeks to answer those questions.

Ignorance of God's word
But if they do not listen, they perish by the sword and die without knowledge.
(Job 36:12).

My people are destroyed for lack of knowledge.
(Hosea 4:6).

We have a responsibility to know the word of God. If I procrastinate or am too lazy to feed on the word and meditate on His promises; lack of knowledge potentially can destroy me and leave me open to continual spiritual attack.
If TV, Facebook, Twitter, our social life etc, has first place over our devotion to the word, our circumstances won't change.
So many of Gods people are bound up, broken, living with long term sickness, and would never think of picking up the word and finding out who they are In Christ, therefore they remain spiritual babies? This has to change because you can't substitute the word of God with anything; it's what brings growth to our spiritual lives.

As newborn babes, desire the pure milk of the word, that you may grow thereby, if indeed you have tasted that the Lord is gracious.
(1 Peter 2-3).

With all your getting, get understanding.
(Proverbs 4:7).

In other words, in all our efforts, make sure that we achieve understanding, that has to be our priority, and the revelation you and I need will come from the inspiration of the scriptures.

I remember reading an article by Charles Spurgeon, who was one of the most famous preachers and writers of the eighteenth century - his books and articles are still popular today. On one occasion, he was visiting the small, impoverished cottage of one of his congregation. She had served all her life as a maid to the Lord and Lady of a famous English Manor, who had now both passed away. She had retired and her eye sight was now partial, and she was unable to read any letters or mail she received. She showed Mr Spurgeon a letter she had, which had been on the mantle piece for two and a half years.

As Mr Spurgeon read the letter, he was alarmed and shocked at the content in the letter, He asked her when she received this letter, she said, two years ago. He then asked her if she was aware of the contents of the letter; her reply was, 'no'. He told her that the Lord and Lady of the manor had left her an inheritance of a beautiful property and enough finance so that she would never be in need for the rest of her life.
Unfortunately, she was unable to live and enjoy the inheritance she had because she was blind and ignorant of what rightfully and legally was hers. This was a tragedy for her, and unfortunately it's a tragedy for many Christians.

We have an inheritance

"So now, brethren, I commend you to God and to the word of his grace, which is able to build you up and give you an inheritance among all those who are sanctified."
(Acts 20:32).

Lack of knowledge destroys us, and disables us in understanding the inheritance we have. Make a fresh commitment to the word today. Meditate on it day and night *(Joshua 1:8-10)*, place it above what you feel, what you see, what you sense, and it will make your life successful and prosper in everything you do.

Unbelief

One of the greatest forces that can work against us is unbelief. Unbelief can cause big problems for Christians, in fact our unbelief can make us miss out on the very things that God has planned for us, this happened to Jesus in his home town of Nazareth.

Jesus said to them, "A prophet is not without honour except in his own country and in his own house." Now He did not do many mighty works there because of their unbelief.
(Matthew 13:57-58).

Jesus was limited in mighty works and miracles, because of their unbelief. The community missed out on the miraculous because they despised Jesus, and questioned who He was and what He could do.

This is one of the reasons that people don't get healed today, truthfully they don't believe that God will do it. They are uncertain whether what God has done for others, He will do for them. That, my friend, is doubt. Doubt is like a wall that stops the power of God flowing into your life.
God will never reward doubt. He rewards faith.
(Hebrews 11:6).

As one preacher said recently, we need to learn to starve our doubts and feed our faith.

"There is nothing impossible with God, all the impossibility is with us, when we measure God by the limitations of our unbelief." - Smith Wigglesworth.

I recently prayed for a gentlemen in a prayer line. He had a long term problem with his arm and He asked me to pray for healing. I asked if he believed Jesus could heal him. To which he responded, "I trust in the sovereignty of God, and if it was his will to heal, He will heal me". Immediately, this gentleman, who had been a Christian for many years, questioned whether God would heal him. He had no faith, and was unsure whether God would answer his prayer or not, and the result; No healing.

Unfortunately, many of us at times are double minded, and double mindedness makes us ineffective in the Kingdom. Double minded in the Greek means a person of two minds, or two souls. Unstable and uncertain in what we believe, and wavering between different opinions. As long as we live like this, we will never learn to have confidence in God and in what He has promised. When we come to God we must ask in faith.

But let him ask in faith, with no doubting, for he who doubts is like a wave of the sea driven and tossed by the wind. For let not that man suppose that he will receive anything from the Lord; he is a double-minded man, unstable in all his ways. (James1:6-8).

Did you notice in verse 6, that it says that we must come to God without any doubting? Because if we doubt we are double minded and we won't receive anything from the Lord. *Romans 12* says that we all have a measure of faith, as the church we are described as the household of faith.
(Galatians 6:10).

That's why we are called believers, because we believe.

Leonard Ravenhill said, "the best title of much of the professing church today, in my judgement is unbelieving believers."

Deal with doubt and unbelief today
Trust in the Lord with all your heart, and lean not on your own understanding?
(Proverbs 3:5).

Trust is the key, therefore, if Gods said it, I am going to believe it, and that settles it.
As Brooke Mcgothlin said, ''if what you feel, and what God says are two different things, you're wrong''. Choose to believe God above everything.

Sin
Sin hinders healing, bitterness, hidden sins. Un-forgiveness, resentment, and many more are like a spiritual poison that can keep people bound in sickness and disease. Sin will hinder our prayers being answered.

Therefore confess your sins to each other and pray for each other so that you may be healed. The prayer of a righteous person is powerful and effective.
(James 5:16).

If we know we have sinned against God, we must confess our sins, for He is always faithful and just to forgive us our sins *(1 John 1:8).* Paul speaks about personal sin concerning communion and the Lord's table. In the church in Corinth there was divisions, drunkenness, gluttony and a despising of the cup of the Lord, which resulted in many being weak, sick and some falling asleep.
(1 Corinthians 11:30).

Listen; deal with sin. It's not your nature and it does not belong in your life.

The demonic
Sometimes sickness is caused by demonic spirits. Demons are evil spirits who seek to find a home in a human body. They are fallen spirits who are evil, and seek to steal, kill and destroy humanity.
In Luke 13, Jesus heals a crippled woman who was bound by a spirit.

On a Sabbath Jesus was teaching in one of the synagogues, and a woman was there who had been crippled by a spirit for eighteen years. She was bent over and could not straighten up at all. When Jesus saw her, he called her forward and said to her, "Woman, you are set free from your infirmity." Then he put his hands on her, and immediately she straightened up and praised God.
Then should not this woman, a daughter of Abraham, whom Satan has kept bound for eighteen long years, be set free on the Sabbath day from what bound her?
(Luke13:10-16).

Disease was caused by evil spirits
After this, Jesus traveled about from one town and village to another proclaiming the good news of the kingdom of God. The Twelve were with him, and also some women who had been cured of evil spirits and diseases.
(Luke 8:1-2).

We can note from these two instances that satan can bind people through sickness. This one woman was bound for eighteen years. Furthermore in *(Luke 8:2)*, we find that evil spirits can be associated with diseases, and cause suffering to a person's life.

We need to understand that we are in a spiritual war, and we don't wrestle with flesh and blood, but powers and principalities in the heavenly places, *(Ephesians 6:12)*.
Praise God that through Jesus, we have victory for He came to destroy the work of the evil one.
He has now given us power and authority over the kingdom of darkness *(1 John 3:8)*, for greater is He that is within us than he that is in the world.
(1 John 4:4).

Once I spoke in a meeting, and I noticed a lady who came in with crutches and could not walk properly, as I was preaching the Holy Spirit instructed me by the word of knowledge that the sickness in her leg was not natural, but caused by a spirit. I stopped speaking and asked her to stand; I rebuked the spirit and commanded it to leave her in Jesus name, and she fell to the floor, by the end of the meeting she was totally healed, after years of suffering.
We should never dismiss the supernatural, because there are many people who are bound by spirits and need to be released by the power of the Holy Spirit.

As believers, the devil has absolutely no power over us when our faith is in Jesus. Our faith in His word and His promises give us power over the enemy to disrupt his plans and purposes.

Behold I give unto you power to tread on serpents and scorpions, and over all the power of the enemy: and nothing shall by any means hurt you.
(Luke 10:19).

As the church, we have power over the enemy, and are called to heal the sick and cast our devil's *(Matthew 10:8)*, whether that be physically, mentally or spiritually.

Wrong Teaching
I don't believe that God punishes His people by putting sickness on them, neither do I believe a distorted view of the sovereignty of God; that God wills everything good or bad to happen to us. That's not the God we serve. We clearly have a will and make choices which sometimes can lead to harm or destruction.
God has a perfect plan for every person's life, *(Jeremiah 29:11)*, but He doesn't make us walk that path like robots. We are free, moral agents with the ability to choose. God has told us what the right choices are, *(Deuteronomy 30:19)*, but He doesn't make those choices for us.

James 4:7 says, "Submit yourselves therefore to God. Resist the devil, and he will flee from you." We must submit to God the things that are of God, and resist the devil. The word "resist" means, "Actively fight against." If we say, "Whatever will be, will be" this is not actively fighting against the devil. We must take a stand against the enemy of our souls, *(Ephesians 6:13),* resist him and watch him flee.

There are Old Testament instances where God smote people with sickness and plagues, because it was punishment for disobedience. But none of those instances were blessings. They were curses. God did use sickness in the Old Testament as punishment, but in the New Testament, Jesus bore our curse for us, *(Galatians 3:13)*. The Lord would no more put sickness on a New Testament believer than He would make us commit a sin. Both forgiveness of sin and healing are a part of the atonement Jesus provided for us.

Deuteronomy, chapter 28, should forever settle this question for all who believe the Word of God. The first 14 verses of Deuteronomy 28, list the blessings of God, and the last 53 verses list the curses. Healing is listed as a blessing *(Deuteronomy. 28:4)*. Sickness is listed as a curse in

Deuteronomy 28:22, 27-28, 35, 59-61. God called sickness a curse. We should not call it a blessing.

There have been many theories regarding Paul's thorn in the flesh which are mentioned in *2 Corinthians 12.* Some have believed that it was sickness or infirmities that God placed on Paul.

"And lest I should be exalted above measure by the abundant of the revelations, a thorn in the flesh was given to me, a messenger of satan to buffet me, lest I be exalted above measure. Concerning this thing I pleaded with the Lord three times that it might depart from me. And He said to me, "My grace is sufficient for you, for My strength is made perfect in weakness." Therefore most gladly I will rather boast in my infirmities, that the power of Christ rest upon me. Therefore I take pleasure in reproaches, in needs, in persecutions, in distresses, for Christ's sake. For when I am weak, then I am strong."
(2 Corinthians 12:7-10).

Paul clearly identifies the thorn as a messenger of satan, therefore demonic in origin.

Andrew Womack gives clear understanding to these verses:
"In verse 7, right after the thorn in the flesh is mentioned, there is a phrase set off by commas which says, "The messenger of Satan to buffet me." This is an explanation of what the thorn was. It was not a thing but rather a demonic messenger. The word used as "messenger" here is always translated as angel or messenger and refers to a created being. So, Paul's thorn was literally a demon sent from Satan to buffet him. The word "buffet" means to strike repeatedly as waves would buffet the shore.
How did this demonic force continually strike Paul? Traditionally it has been taught that it was with sickness, and the thing that made many accept that is the use of the words "weakness" and "infirmity" in verses 9 and 10. Infirmity

definitely does mean sickness and is used that way in 1 Timothy 5:23, but that is not the only meaning of the word. The number two definition is any lack or inadequacy. For instance, Romans 8:26 says, "the Spirit also helpeth our infirmities." In this case, the context makes it clear that it is not speaking of sicknesses but rather not knowing what to pray for. Our finite minds are an infirmity, or an inadequacy."

"If we look at the context of Paul's thorn in the flesh, we find that infirmity does not mean sickness in 2 Corinthians 12:9 and 10. In 2 Corinthians 11:30, Paul uses the exact terminology of "glorying in infirmities" that is used just a few verses later in speaking about this thorn. In the eleventh chapter he had just finished listing what those infirmities were. In verses 23-29, he lists such things as imprisonment, stripes, shipwrecks, and stoning's; none of these speak of sickness. Verse 27 mentions weakness and painfulness, which some have tried to make mean sickness, but it is just as possible he could have been weary and suffered painfulness from such things as being stoned and left for dead (Acts 14:19). All these things listed in 2 Corinthians 11, refer to persecutions as infirmities. So, in context, Paul's thorn was a demonic angel or messenger sent by Satan which continually stirred up persecution against him. This is also verified by three Old Testament references (Num. 33:55; Josh. 23:13 and Judg. 2:3), where people are spoken of as being "thorns in your sides" and "thorns in your eyes.""

Chapter 9

The Weapons of our Warfare.

The weapons of our warfare

For the weapons of our warfare are not carnal but mighty in God for pulling down strongholds.
(2 Corinthians 10:4).

God has given us spiritual weapons to pull down and demolish all the demonic strongholds that stand against us, as the church of Jesus Christ. We must have full assurance in the finished work of the cross and realise.

That greater is He that is within us than He that is in the world.
(1 John 4:4).

Recognition of what we have is vital for the believer, so that we can live the life of one who is more than a conqueror.

The prayer of faith

Prayer is clearly connected to healing. The first instance we find of healing in the bible is because of prayer.

So Abraham prayed to God; and God healed Abimelech, his wife, and his female servants. Then they bore children; for the Lord had closed up all the wombs of the house of Abimelech because of Sarah, Abraham's wife.
(Genesis 20:17).

Abraham prayed and God healed. Prayer was essential then and prayer is essential now.

And the prayer of faith will restore the one who is sick, and the Lord will raise him up; and if he has committed sins, he will be forgiven. Therefore, confess your sins to one another (your false steps, your offences), and pray for one another, that you may be healed and restored. The heartfelt and persistent prayer of a righteous man (believer) can accomplish much (when put into action and made effective by God—it is dynamic and can have tremendous power).
(James 5:15-16 amplified).

Every prayer which we pray is powerful and effective, but it must be a prayer of faith, for without faith it's impossible to please God, *(Hebrews 11:6)*. We must have complete trust in the God of Heaven.
The prayer of faith is dynamic and has tremendous power. It promises to restore the sick person to health; Jesus also told us to have faith in God constantly. The bible does not teach us to have faith or belief in God when the crisis arrive's, or when the spiritual climate looks good. No, it's a lifestyle we are called to live, as the bible declares that the just or righteous shall live by faith. In fact, this verse is repeated four times in the bible, which shows the priority God places upon faith.
(Habakkuk 2:4), (Romans 1:17), (Galatians 3:11), (Hebrews 10:38).

Our prayer of faith in God will move any and every mountain of sickness or disease that affects our lives. Therefore, it's essential to trust God and live by faith, so that every attack and stronghold of the enemy can be extinguished.

Above all, lift up the (protective) shield of faith with which you can extinguish all the flaming arrows of the evil one.
(Ephesians 6:16).

Having complete trust in the God of Heaven when we pray, causes Jehovah to move Heaven and Earth on your behalf and put your miracle into motion.

For everyone born of God overcomes the world. This is the victory that has overcome the world, even our faith. (1 John 5:4).

If your struggling to believe God on your own, find a man or woman of faith and get into agreement with them. Ask them to lay hands on you, so you can recover, *(Mark 16:18)*, because two are better than one, *(Ecclesiastes 4:9-12)* If you're sick the bible is clear that you can call for your leaders to anoint you with oil and pray the prayer of faith and you will be healed, *(James 5:13-15).*

We need each other because one might put a thousand to flight, but two will put ten thousand to flight. There is power in numbers, and there is power in agreement, and a unity of faith. Anna and I will always try and pray together for others, as we believe that by praying, there is power released through our agreement together.

"Again I say to you that if two of you agree on earth concerning anything that they ask, it will be done for them by My Father in heaven. (Matthew 18:19).

The name of Jesus
There is power in the name of Jesus, for everything in heaven, earth and hell has to bow and submit to the name of Jesus. That name has authority over satan and his entire kingdom.

Therefore God also has highly exalted Him and given Him the name which is above every name, that at the name of Jesus every knee should bow, of those in heaven, and of those on earth, and of those under the earth. (Philippians 2:9-10).

Jesus left his name with us when He went to heaven, His name is highly exalted, and is above the name of cancer, blindness, arthritis, fear and every other name and demon. All names must bow to the name above all names Jesus Christ.

In His name, we cast out demons, *(Mark 16:17)*, in His name, Peter commanded healing to the lame man at the gate, Beautiful.

Then Peter said, "Silver and gold I do not have, but what I do have I give you: In the name of Jesus Christ of Nazareth, rise up and walk." And he took him by the right hand and lifted him up, and immediately his feet and ankle bones received strength. So he, leaping up, stood and walked and entered the temple with them—walking, leaping, and praising God. (Acts 3:6-8).

His name has power and authority over all sickness.
Smith Wigglesworth, on one occasion, was asked to visit the home a man, who was dying of tuberculosis. As he stood at his bedside with a group of men, they made a circle around the bed, and declared one word over the man again. That was Jesus, Jesus, Jesus. Initially, nothing happened. They continued to declare that name Jesus, and as they did, the power of God fell, the bed shook and the man was made perfectly whole, because there is all power and all authority in that name. We have a right to pray and ask in that name.

And whatever you ask in My name, that I will do, that the Father may be glorified in the Son. If you ask anything in My name, I will do it.
(John 14:13-14).

"And in that day you will ask Me nothing. Most assuredly, I say to you, whatever you ask the Father in My name He will give you. Until now you have asked nothing in My name. Ask, and you will receive, that your joy may be full.
(John 16:23-24).

According to these verses, we have a right to ask the father for healing in Jesus name, He says whatever we ask in his name, the father will give it to you, so that he alone is glorified. We have been given the legal right and divine privilege to use his name. The name of Jesus is like a signed cheque, that releases all the resources of heaven. All we have to do is ask in His name.

The authority of the word
The word is a revelation of God's will for all of us; therefore, it has to have first priority and final authority. Everything around us has been framed or brought into existence by the word of God ,*(Hebrews 11:6)*, and that the whole of creation is still being upheld by the word of His power, *(Hebrews 1:3)*. If this is the case, the word must have first place in my life and your life.

This Book of the Law shall not depart from your mouth, but you shall meditate in it day and night, that you may observe to do according to all that is written in it. For then you will make your way prosperous, and then you will have good success.
(Joshua 1:8).

We've got to do what God told Joshua to do and that is to meditate on this word day and night, until we've taken it in to our hearts. Meditation in the Hebrew means to chew over the word just like the cow would do with the cud. Continually chewing it until all the nutrients have been absorbed. We have got to do that until this word and the promises in this book open the eyes of our understanding and clearly become a part of our lives.

Let the word of Christ dwell in you richly.
(Col 3 v 16).

We must become saturated in the bible, we have to devour the book and it's truths to live in us, in abundance, as we do the truths within shall set us free.

I have, for the last twenty years, had a problem with my feet; I have been to the doctors over many years to receive many different types of medicine, but never experienced healing. A few months ago, I made a decision to place the word of God above my symptoms and believe it had power and authority over all sickness in my body. I started to believe *(Proverbs 3:1)*, which says to not forget His law, and keep the commandments of his word, for it will be healing for my flesh and strength for my bones.

I gave attention to the word, believed it, confessed it and gave thanks for what God had promised. Within a few weeks my feet were completely healed, I did not have hands laid on me, or travelled around the world to a revival meeting. No, I took hold of the word, believed it for myself and got completely healed. What worked for me will work for you, because God's word is His will and it has final authority on everything.

The power of the Holy Spirit
We must take note of the last words of Jesus, which He spoke before He left the earth, for they are vital to note.

But you shall receive power when the Holy Spirit has come upon you; and you shall be witnesses to Me in Jerusalem, and in all Judea and Samaria, and to the end of the earth."
(Acts 1:8).

We must be a people who rely totally on the Spirit, for the Holy Spirit is the power of God, who brings a manifestation of the promises. It's His anointing that breaks every type of sickness and bondage. Just like Jesus, we are anointed with the same Holy Spirit, that anointing of the Spirit is upon us to enforce

Christ's victory and remove all trace of sickness from people's lives, for that is what Jesus did.

How God anointed Jesus of Nazareth with the Holy Spirit and with power, who went about doing good and healing all who were oppressed by the devil, for God was with Him. (Acts 10:38).

The same call upon Jesus is upon us, and that is to heal all that are oppressed by the devil, not some but all sickness and all disease, this will only be achieved by the Holy Spirit.

For it will never be by might, nor by power but by my Spirit says the Lord.
(Zechariah 4:6).

Renewing of the mind
The greatest battles for many people are not the external battles, but the internal battle. The mind can be one of the hardest areas to control, and remains one of the greatest challenges for the believer. But it can be controlled and renewed, and we can have the mind of Christ.
(1 Corinthians 2:16).

I don't want satan or the circumstances of life controlling my mind, I want the word of God controlling my thought life, for that renews me and brings total transformation.

Do not be shaped by (conformed to; pressed into a mould by) this world (age); instead be changed within (transformed) by a new way of thinking (or changing the way you think; the renewing of your mind). Then you will be able to decide (discern; test and approve) what God wants for you (is God's will); you will know what is good and pleasing to him and what is perfect.
(Romans 12:2-3 EXB).

God wants to change us through the ongoing daily process of renewing our minds. Daily commitment to God's word will cause us to see ourselves from God's perspective and be transformed. *Proverbs 23:7 says, "As a man thinks in his heart, so is he."* I like to say it like this: Where the mind goes, the man follows. We are what we think; therefore anything that contradicts his word can be changed through renewing our minds.

Let God shape your thoughts, and decide to think on the right things. Those thoughts that are divine, God filled, and shaped by the authority of His word, rather than those which are full of negativity, despair and hopelessness.

Think only about (Set your minds on; Fix your thoughts on) the things in heaven (above), not the things on earth. (For) Your old sinful self has (You) died, and your new life is kept (hidden) with Christ in God.
(Colossians 3:2 EXB).

(Finally; In conclusion; or Now then) Brothers and sisters, think about (focus your thoughts on; fill your minds with) things that are true and honourable and right (just) and pure and beautiful (lovely) and respected (commendable). If there is anything that is good (morally excellent) and worthy of praise, ·think about (focus your thoughts on; fill your minds with) these things.
(Philippians 4:8 EXB).

It's time to set our minds on what God thinks about us, and allow the word and the Spirit to remove any negative mindsets that we have concerning healing. This will take time but it can be done, as we allow God to awaken our minds to the truth that has the power to set us free.
(John 8:32).

Chapter 10

The Victorious Church.

I will build My church, and the gates of Hades shall not prevail against it. And I will give you the keys of the kingdom of heaven, and whatever you bind on earth will be bound in heaven, and whatever you loose on earth will be loosed in heaven."
(Matthew 16:18-19).

Jesus gave us the promise that He would build his church, and hell would not prevail or have power over it. He said, what we would bind in heaven would be bound on Earth.
We are part of a victorious church that are called not only to be healed, but to minister the same healing power of Jesus to the world around us, for we are Jesus to our world.

As He is, so are we in this world.
(1 John 4:17).

That means that what Jesus did when he walked the earth, we are to do today, for signs, wonders and miracles did not end with Jesus ministry, they are to continue through His church today.
From the youngest to the oldest, we are a representation of Jesus to our generation, for the same anointing that was upon Jesus is upon us, to bring his healing power to broken humanity.
What Jesus declared and lived in, we now carry and walk in.

"The Spirit of the Lord is upon Me (the Messiah), Because He has anointed Me to preach the good news to the poor.

*He has sent Me to announce release (pardon, forgiveness) to
the captives,
And recovery of sight to the blind,
To set free those who are oppressed (downtrodden, bruised,
crushed by tragedy),
to proclaim the favourable year of the Lord (the day when
salvation and the favour of God abound greatly)."
(Luke 4:18-19 EXB).*

As the anointing was on the messiah, it's also on you and me,
we are anointed to preach and share the gospel. We are sent
to bring release to captives, sight to the blind, and to set free
those who are oppressed. This is our calling, and this is our
commission.

I remember listening to Bill Johnson, give a testimony from a
mother in his church. She was in a supermarket, and her
daughter was with her, as they were walking down one of the
aisle's the daughter said to her mum, "there's a lady in a
wheel chair at the bottom of the isle and Jesus wants to heal
her". The mother questioned her, and the child said that she
saw Jesus standing behind the lady saying He wanted to heal
her. They went and told the lady that God wanted to heal her,
and the young child laid her hands on the lady and
immediately she was healed. God is no respecter of persons,
neither is He of age.

I believe that God wants to use us all uniquely like that, for the
anointing of the Spirit is not for meetings or confined to a
church building. It's our commission is to take the power of the
gospel which saves and heals and delivers into this lost and
broken world. We have to stop being ashamed of the gospel,
because it is the power of God unto salvation, *(Romans 1:16).*
We are not witnesses, if we just proclaim him within the
context of a church meeting; no we are to be witnesses for
him at home, in the workplace, in the supermarket, at the
petrol station and whenever and wherever we have an
opportunity to release His word and his power.

Heal the sick, cleanse the lepers, raise the dead, cast out demons. Freely you have received, freely give. (Matthew 10:8).

And He said to them, "Go into all the world and preach the gospel to every creature. He who believes and is baptised will be saved; but he who does not believe will be condemned. And these signs will follow those who believe: In My name they will cast out demons; they will speak with new tongues; they will take up serpents; and if they drink anything deadly, it will by no means hurt them; they will lay hands on the sick, and they will recover." (Mark 16:15-18).

Whether you are a housewife, a businessman, a student or retired, this is your commission and mandate as a believer. Our goal and desire has to be more than just receiving healing, that would be selfish and self centred on our behalf. It has to be to take His healing power to the world in which we live. Jesus did not say for the church to wait for the world to come to us, that never has and never will happen. He said go into the world, heal the sick, raise the dead, preach the gospel, and lay hands on those who are ill, and they shall recover.

I pray that as you are healed reading this book, that you to will see yourself as an ambassador for Christ, *(2 Corinthians 5:20).* A minister of the gospel anointed with the power of the Holy Spirit, ready to be a part of winning your generation to Christ.
(Mark 16:15-18), (Luke 4:16-18).

#0252 - 190218 - C0 - 210/148/4 - PB - DID2126469